Stories From The Rock

Cracking the myth of Es Vedra, Ibiza

LUCIEN LECARME

Published in 2020 by Lucien Lecarme / IbizaPowerspot
Copyright Lucien Lecarme
Cover Design : Lucien Lecarme
Cover Photo: Lucien Lecarme, all rights reserved

Lucien Lecarme has asserted his rights to be identified as the author of this book in accordance with the Copy-right, Designs and Patents Act 1988

All Rights Reserved

No part of this publication may be reproduced, stored in retrieval system, or transmitted in any form or by any means, electronic, mechanical, photocopying, recording or otherwise, without the prior permission of the copy-right owner

www.ibizapowerspot.com/storiesfromtherock

This book is dedicated to Es Vedra, the magical, mythical and sacred Rock in the south east of Ibiza. I had the absolute honour to live in front of 'The Rock' for 7 years.

I admired 'her' while doing yoga on my rooftop. I experienced her magnetic pull at first hand. Like the Goddess Tanit in the north, Es Vedra protects the island and its inhabitants, by holding space for our personal processes, by accelerating them, and by charging us and Ibiza with enchanted beauty and magic.

In a rapidly changing world, where technology is taking over, we need our sacred sanctuaries more than ever. Our places to pray, meditate and feel nurtured and interconnected through a direct connection to the elements.

Es Vedra is a place where you can move out of time for a moment and be found on the other side of infinity. A place to spiral back towards the beginning. To rebirth into our new era of unity, love and connection.

This book is my tribute to Es Vedra.

Lucien Lecarme

Author of the futurenovel 'The Wisdom Keeper"
Blogger & Founder of Earth WIsdom Tribe

www.medium.com/@lucienlecarme
lucien@ibizapowerspot.com

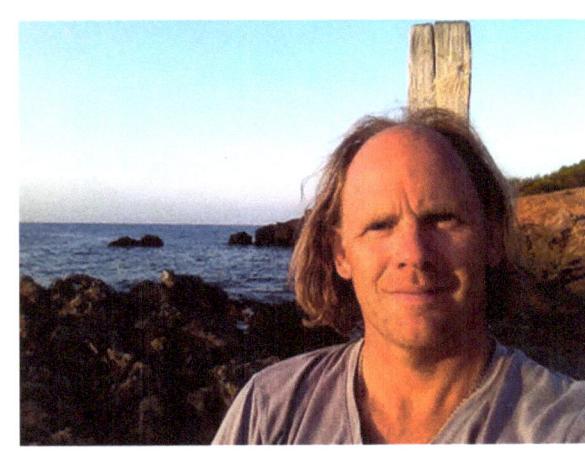

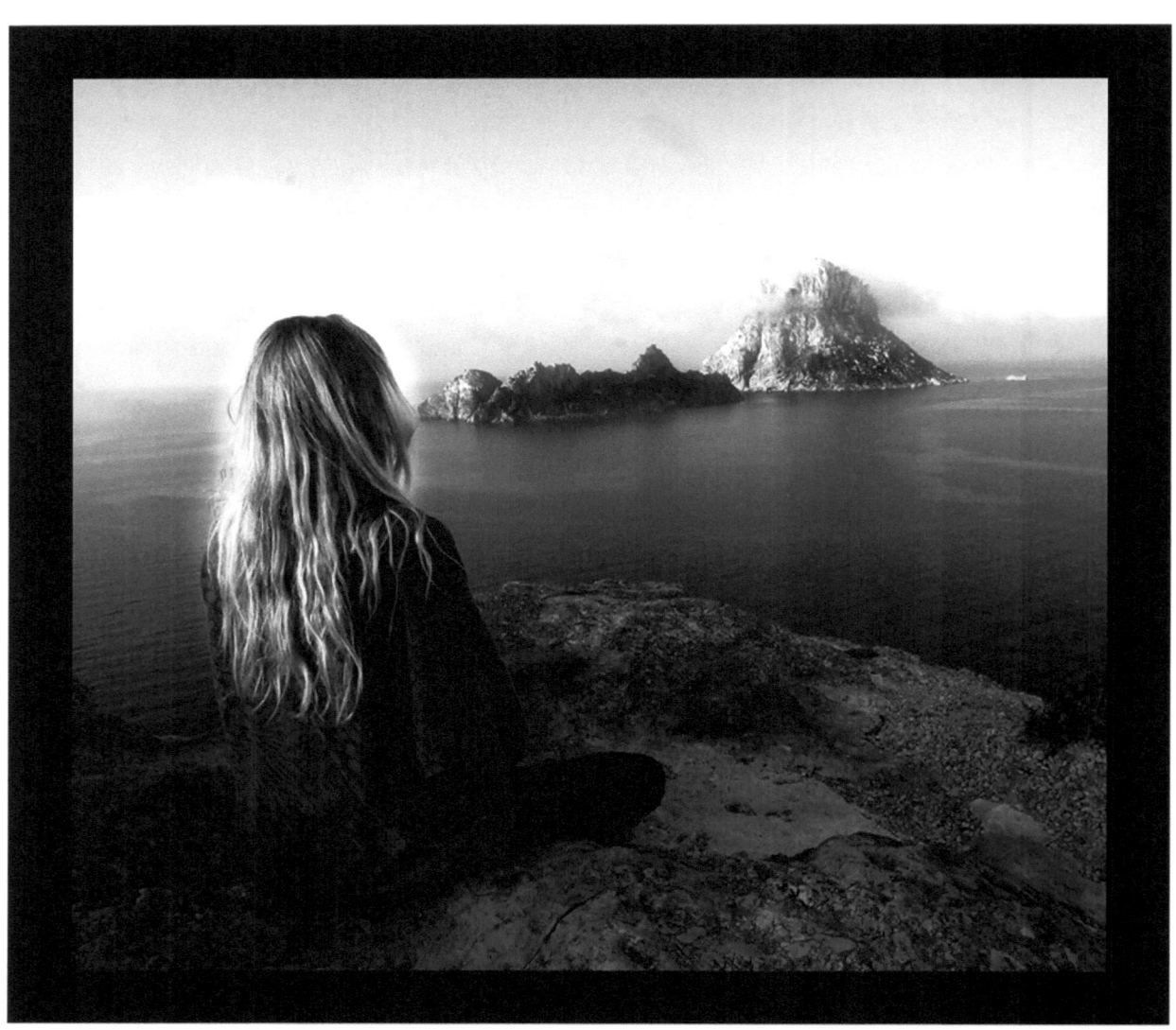

contents

Intro

A magnetic spell or sirens singing?

Padre Palua

Undefined Flying Objects

The resurrection of the Goats of Es Vedra

Artists and the Rock

Es Vedra: A Tectonic Monument

Spiral Dance

A spiritual pull

More stories from the Rock

Discovering the magical Island of Ibiza in 2012 for the first time felt like visiting an old friend. Immediately I felt at home. When you have ever visited the island, you might recognize the feeling. I felt such an amazing strong pull towards this hub of creative people, abundant nature, amazing pristine beaches, radio stations with 24/7 smooth EDM without commercials and 300 days of sun. Not to forget the special light and fabulous sunsets that must have cast a spell on the first artist arriving on the island more than half a decade ago. They couldn't leave too and decided to stay.

A magical wave pulled me away from my career and certainties in Holland, dropping me in front of Es Vedra, the magnetic landmark and tourist hot spot. Es Vedra is a 386 meters high Sphinx-like rock formation that once belonged to the mainland. It separated, and now the story goes it safeguards the island together with it's smaller brother, Es Vedranell.

Some people claim it's the exact opposite of the caves of Tanit in the North near Cala St. Vicente. Imagine Ibiza as a Pancake folded in two, Vedra now touches the entrance of the cave with its stony head. These two heroic opposites symbolize the masculine and the feminine energy present on Ibiza.

Friends visiting seeing the rock for the first time nodd in disbelief. They tell me things like; "It looks like that rock is carved out in the sky, it just ain't real". Others have a moment in silence to take in the sublime beauty of yet another sunset that casts its beauty over the rock and the island. Many people come to the cliffs in front of Es Vedra to meditate, or just have a moment for themselves.

People on the sunset platform in the natural parque of Cala d'Hort in summer applaud every single night in awe. They suddenly feel themselves part of an age old ritual of honouring the sun, life, yet another day on this amazing planet. They are probably not aware that thousands of people from many different cultures did the exact same thing on Ibiza, a place for celebration.

Seven years ago, Es Vedra pulled me to its doorstep. I accepted the invitation to live In front of a place with so much power, myth and especially stories. From the downright unbelievable to the flat mundane. Here are 10 stories of the Rock. From old Ibicencan people that claim there is a monster lurking in some of it's dark caves, to tourists that need a selfie with the rock to make their holiday complete.

Is Es Vedra a UFO landing place? Is it built on crystals and the waters around have infinite depth? Is a powerful dragon hiding inside? Is it a magnificent Powerspot where higher programs for humanity enter the earth?

It is time to crack the myth.

1. Magnetic Spell or Sirens Singing?

It is commonly well known that Es Vedra is the third magnetic place in the world. FInding scientific proof for this is hard, but this book does not aim on 'proving' anything, rather than telling appealing stories about a rock that became a legend.

Living in front of the rock, I have heard literally hundreds of friends, visitors, hiking clients or just random tourists, expressing their own unique relationship with Es Vedra. The common denominator is the 'love at first sight' experience. Many Vedra-Virgins tell me they were literally struck by the majestic beauty of this natural monument when they saw it for the first time. This usually happens when people pass the last bend of the road towards Cala Dhort.

A vast blue sea suddenly stretches in front of you, after the bend, there he or she is. For me, it's a He, since the rock has a kind of fallus shape and is commonly referred to as having a lot of masculine energy. In contrast to the caves on the complete other end of the island, near Cala Dt. Vicente. There you'll find the Tanit Caves, named after the protector Goddess of the island. More of her later.

So there he appears on the left side. In all his masculinity. Not just a rock, but a powerful presence hard to miss. A few friends told me they literally felt as if something hit them in the belly. Many people describe the rock generating a strong magnetic pulse, comparable to places like Stonehenge, Easter Island or the Egyptian Pyramids. When the myth of being the third magnetic place on earth is real, the consequence is that the only two places more magnetic are the North Pole and the Bermuda Triangle.

It is safe to say that seeing Es Vedra for the first time in your life, is a breathtaking experience. All of this love expressed for the rock, all of the personal stories people have, all the magic that I had the honor of experiencing almost everyday, all of that inspired me to write this book using my best photos I took over the years. Rain and shine.

Not many people know this, but Es Vedra is part of a mediteranian triangle of magnetism, also referred to as the triangle of silence. This triangle is formed by drawing a straight line between the rock of Ifach in Calpe, Alicante all the way to the southwest coast of Mallorca near Pequera. From there the line goes to Es Vedra and back to Ifach. Many Ibicencan and Mallorcan fishermen boats have gone down in the "Silence Triangle". There are numerous reports of engine failure, radars that stop to work and doves becoming disoriented. This is very similar to stories from the Bermuda triangle.

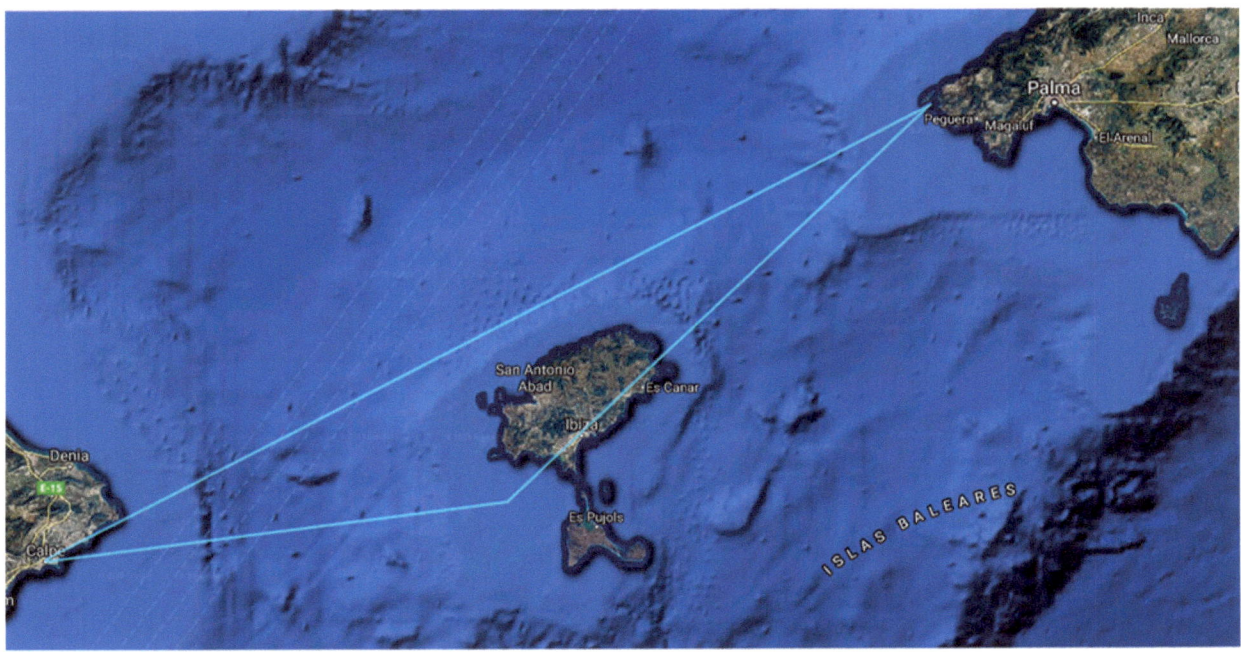

It was not only through this strong magnetic pulse that captains lost their track, compasses went berserk or engines of yachts wouldn't start again. There is another much greater, older and stronger story. The story of the Sirens in Homer's Odyssey. Es Vedra is connected to this ancient Greek mythological masterpiece.

In Homer's epic Greek tale, Odysseus can't resist the pull of the legendary Sirens. They lure sailors into their deaths by their magical songs. Odysseus came up with a plan to be able to hear the hypnotizing angelic siren's voices and live to tell. He ordered his shipmates to tie him to the mast and plug their ears with beeswax. The plan succeeded and Odysseus survived the Siren's songs.

The combination of the magnetism around Es Vedra and the story of the Siren's songs make some Ibicencan sailors avoid the waters around the rock. There is also a very practical reason for this, Es Vedra and his smaller protector and brother Es Vedranell create unpredictable currents with their position. Many times I have seen contradictionary currents arising from the few hundreds meter space between Vedra and Vedranell.

Es Vedra, with its magnetic powers, attracts the skies, divides the waters and lures unprepared tourist yachts and smaller boats into problems. Happily, many were able to live to tell, like Homer, about the strange but beautiful noises they heard surrounding the Island at the moment their engine stopped working. Especially at the West point where a small light tower has been built. A perfect hideout for some sailor hungry Sirens.

Image next page: Ulysses Odysseus and the Sirens by Herbert James Draper. (Public Domain)

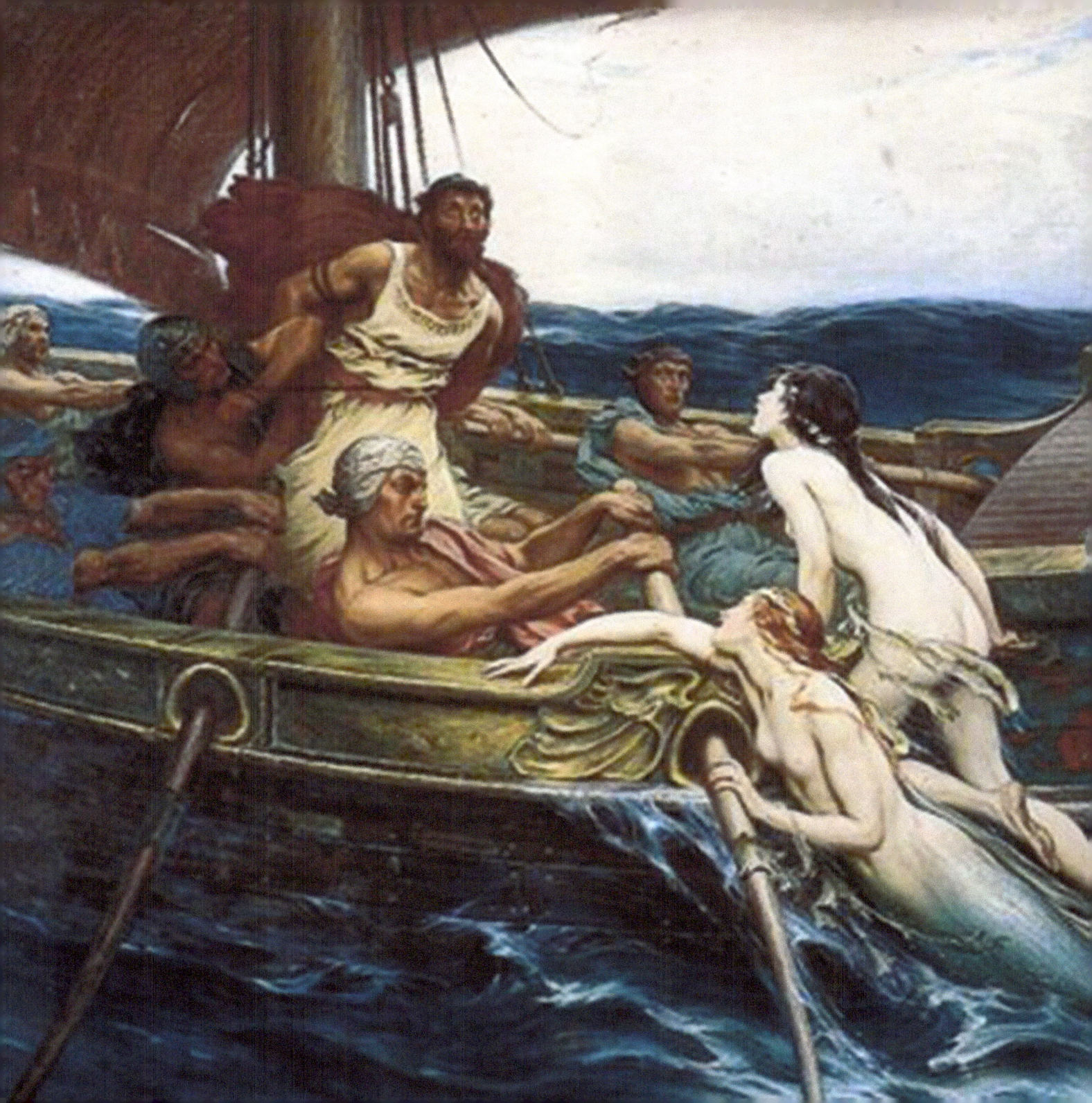

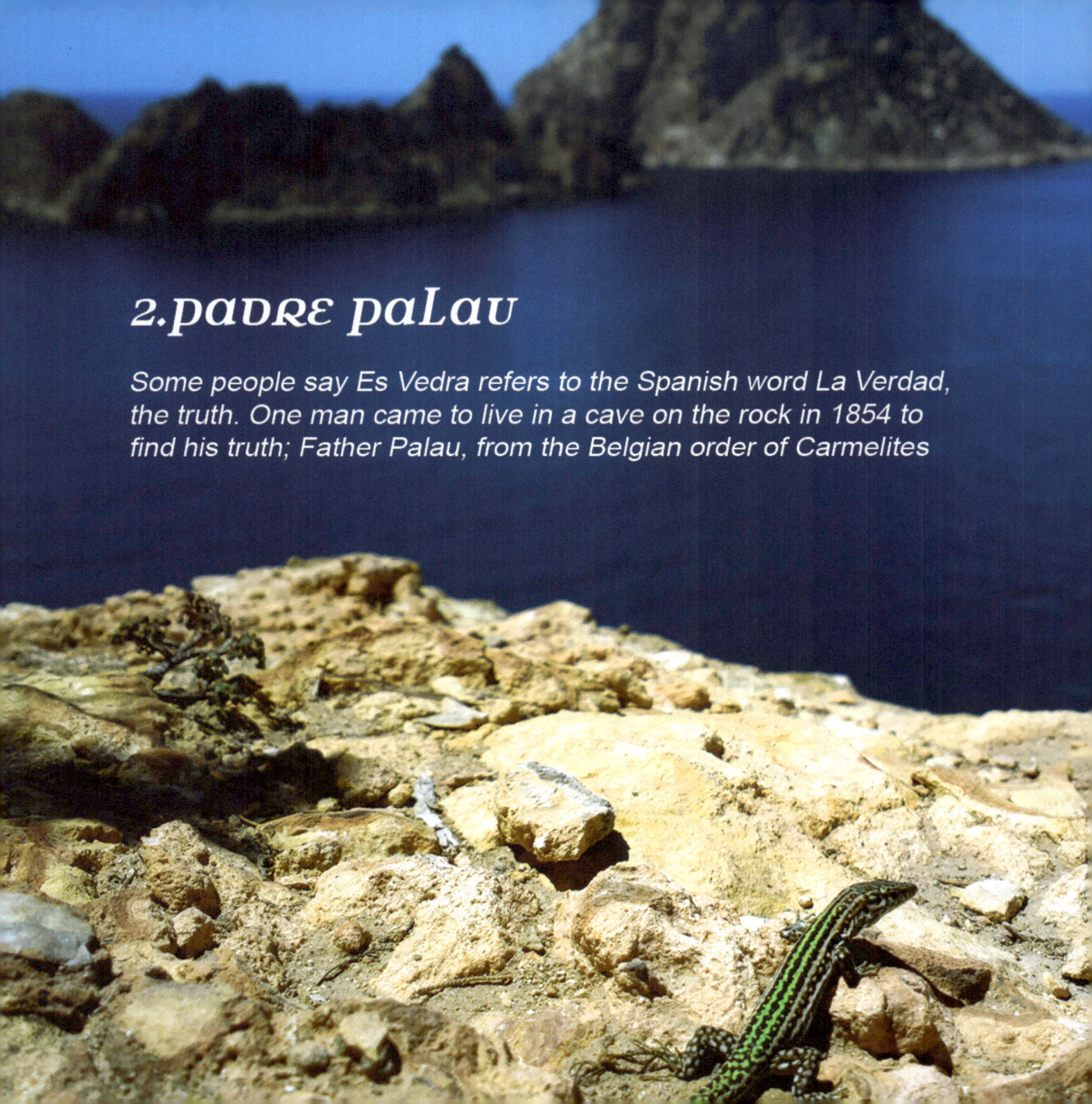

2. Padre Palau

Some people say Es Vedra refers to the Spanish word La Verdad, the truth. One man came to live in a cave on the rock in 1854 to find his truth; Father Palau, from the Belgian order of Carmelites

The story of Father Palau and his life on the rock is undoubtedly the start of Es Vedra becoming a myth. Francisco Palau y Quer, popularly known as Father Palau, was born in 1811 in Catalunya. He got exiled to the island in 1854, when he was only 43. At that time, he was teaching workers catechism in the parish of Sant Agusti in Barcelona. He also taught them the importance of fighting for their justice by means of strike. That got the parish into problems, and they agreed to send Padra Palau to the main prison of Spain at that time, Ibiza. Hard to believe they used the beautiful island of Ibiza as a place of exile, but understand it was a hard life back in those days with only farmers, fishermen and salt workers surviving the constant pirate attacks. No clubs or villa's back in those days, only the resilient sun.

Padre Palau was caught by the beauty of the Rock Es Vedra, and during his first expedition, he found a cave that suited his needs. He created a bed out of sand, that he transported all the way from the base of the rock. He chose that cave, since not far apart he discovered another cave with fresh water dripping from its ceiling.

Imagine this man in exile sitting next to his fire at the entrance of 'his' cave, looking over the sea and feeling blessed by the many stars at night. He never stayed longer than 10 days in the years between 1858 – 1866. One day, Maria revealed herself to him in front of his cave.

He never came back.

Instead, he formed the congregation of Es Cubells, resulting in the Carmelite Monastery of Es Cubells. In the slopes behind the Church of Es Cubells, Padre Palau found another cave to pray and spent time and he created a hermitage there. It is impossible to see Es Vedra, but I am sure he was able to feel the heartbeat of the Rock from that slope overlooking the magnificent curve of Es Cubells all the way towards Cala Llintrisca. Padra Palau started making drawings and small paintings of the Cala Dhort and Es Cubells area, and also impressions of the Rock. In one of those drawings, he calls Es Vedra; " The small mountain of Montserrat ", named after the holy Catalonian Mountain 60km away from Barcelona, famous for it's Black Madonna.

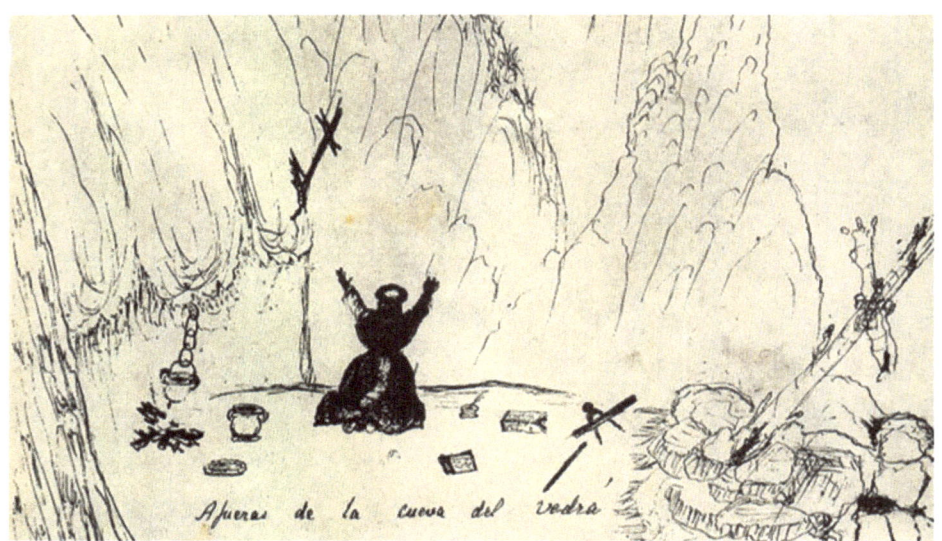

Self Portrait of Father Palau standing outside of his Vedra Cave, praying. Maybe the same place he witnessed the appearance of Maria

Padre Palau's congregation grew worldwide. Over the course of years, Es Vedra became a holy land for more than 2000 missionaries arriving from over 250 communities and 39 countries. For them, the pilgrimage was somehow what Mecca represents for Muslims. The difference is that Mecca is not there to be climbed.

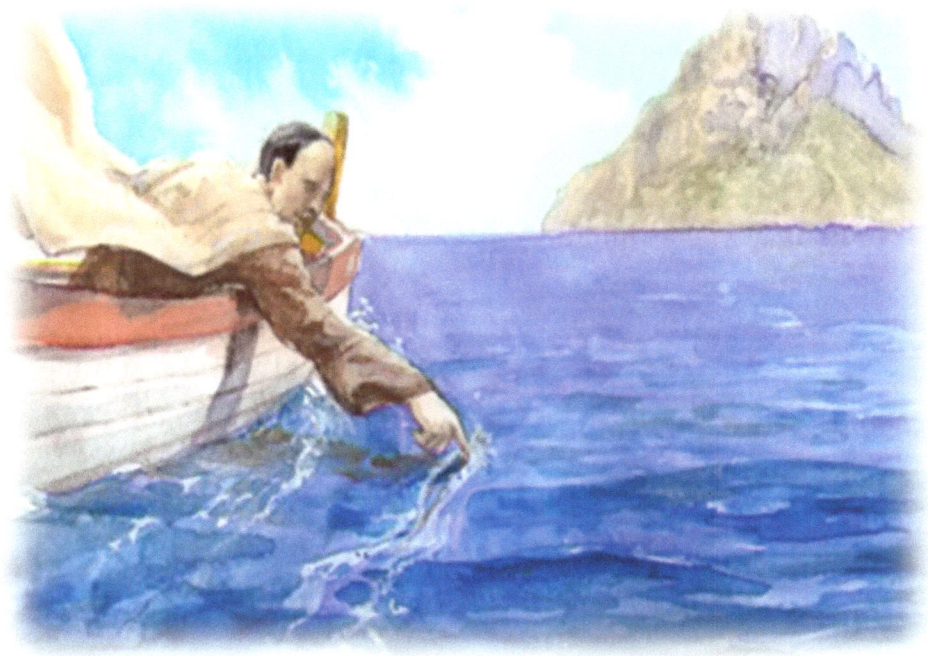

Palau on his way to isolation on the Island of truth: Es Vedra. Source Public Domain

Climbing the islet is a complicated excursion due to the difficulty of the rock. There are no trails and it is necessary to climb with the help of expert climbers. Therefore, although for the Carmelites it was their dream, only a few actually achieved it. In these modern days, a special permit is required to set foot on the holy land for the Carmelites.

This hermit Palau, who found refuge on the island, was Blessed by the Vatican on April 24, 1988. His followers are now waiting for a miracle, for Padre Palau becoming Saint Palau. For them, this is only a matter of time, a matter of praying and believing. Probably what reaching the summit of Vedra must have felt like for the most courageous Carmelites.

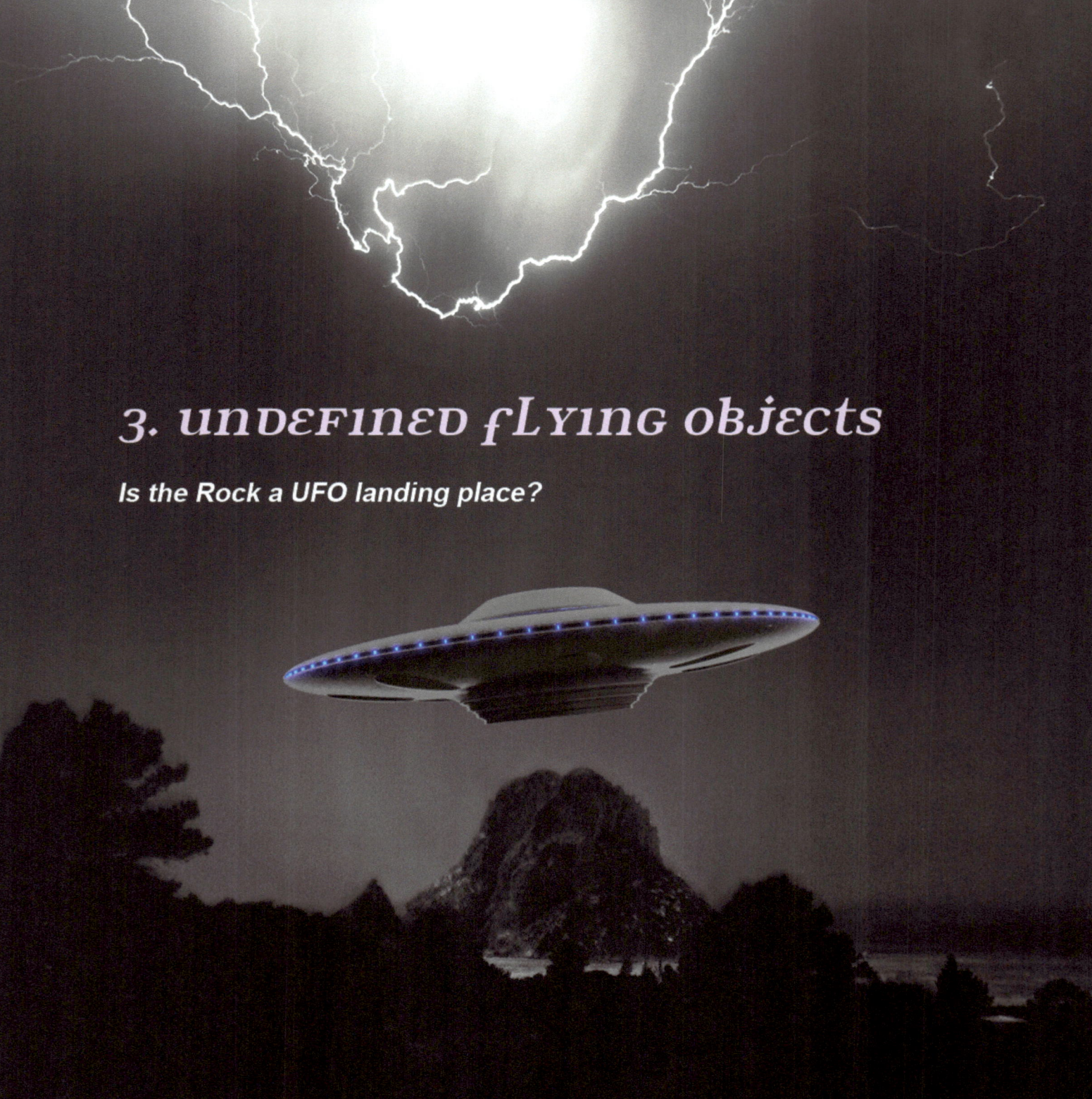

3. Undefined Flying Objects

Is the Rock a UFO landing place?

This claim comes from Swiss author Erich von Däniken, a famous Ufologist who wrote dozens of books about aliens and their spacecraft. His work revolves around the belief that 'ancient astronauts', or extraterrestrials, visited earth and influenced early human culture. The places or objects that relate to this ET contact, often include powerful magnetism. With this in mind, it is not that far-fetched that Von Däniken mentions Es Vedra.

He published his most famous book in 1968: Chariots of the Gods. Von Däniken beliefs structures like the Egyptian pyramids, Stonehenge and the Moai of Easter Island represent higher technological knowledge. He tries to prove that the cultures that lived in those times didn't have the tools, expertise, nor technology to build those complex, mysterious structures.

These theories are far more widely accepted now than in the early seventies. Von Däniken wrote many books about alien life, mostly referring to Paleo contact. This idea claims our ancestors were dummies. Only with the help of intelligent extraterrestrials visiting in prehistoric times, we have been able to create our modern cultures, technologies and religions.

Is there any proof that hyper-intelligent people visited Es Vedra?
The legacy of Padre Palau shows us nothing in that direction. Also, no photos or videos are circulating the Internet with aliens having a well deserved holiday on the Rock.

Von Däniken sold a staggering 63 million books worldwide, making him adopt a playboy lifestyle. Spending one year in jail for forgery didn't slow him down. I can imagine him visiting Ibiza in his playboy years, becoming fascinated by the Rock, its magnetic pulse and mysterious radiation. The paleo contact authority added Es Vedra to his list of first contact places while sipping a cocktail under a palm tree at Cala d'Hort. Who knows?

What we do know is something that comes very close to actual proof of extraterrestrial contact near Es Vedra. 'El Caso Manises' is the story of the most critical and first official UFO sighting in the history of aviation in Spain.

On November 11th, 1979, a tourist plane with 109 passengers on board set off from Palma de Mallorca towards its destination Tenerife. Still reaching for its base height, above Es Vedra, the pilots spotted red lights above the Rock. The mysterious lights started to approach and haunt the aeroplane. This rare phenomenon left them no other choice than making an emergency landing at the nearest Airport, Manises in Valencia. Different people testified the object was at least 200 meters wide.

Many stories, legends and myths surrounding Es Vedra tell of a higher intelligent life force visiting the Rock. When there are just enough of them, some might actually be true. These stories originate from hippies getting stoned on Cala d'Hort beach, staring into the lights of the many moving masts of sailing boats that anchor in the sometimes rocky waters. For them, it's UFO's flying around. Who cares?

One thing is for sure though, these red boat lights were way too far off for the sober pilots of the 1979 flight from Palma de Mallorca to abort their flight schedule. And they don't sound stoned when you listen to the original communication audio. Just google 'El Caso Manises', and you'll see original photos too!

Without any shadow of a doubt, for the captain and the 109 onboard, Es Vedra had an alien visit that remarkable night.

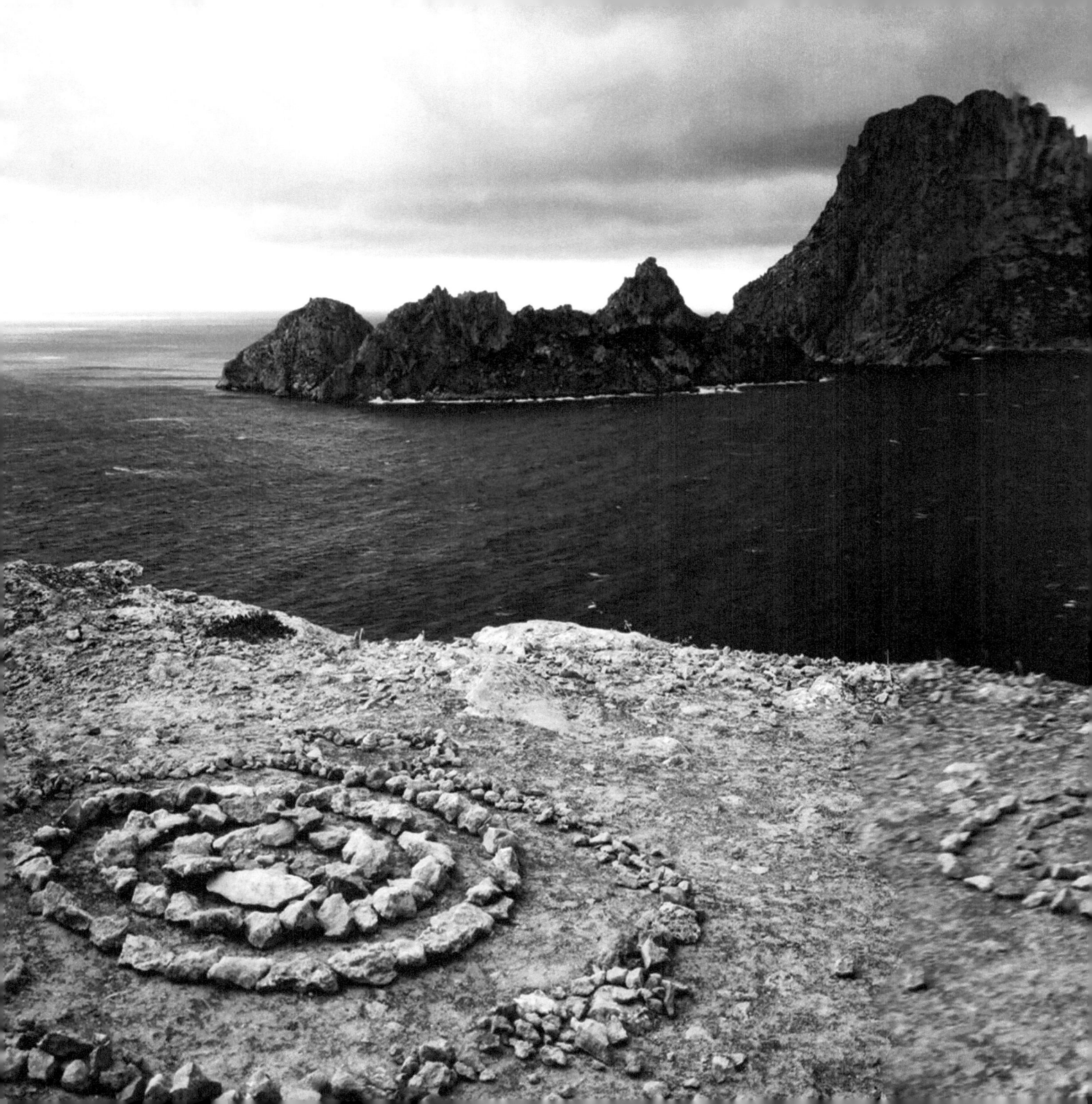

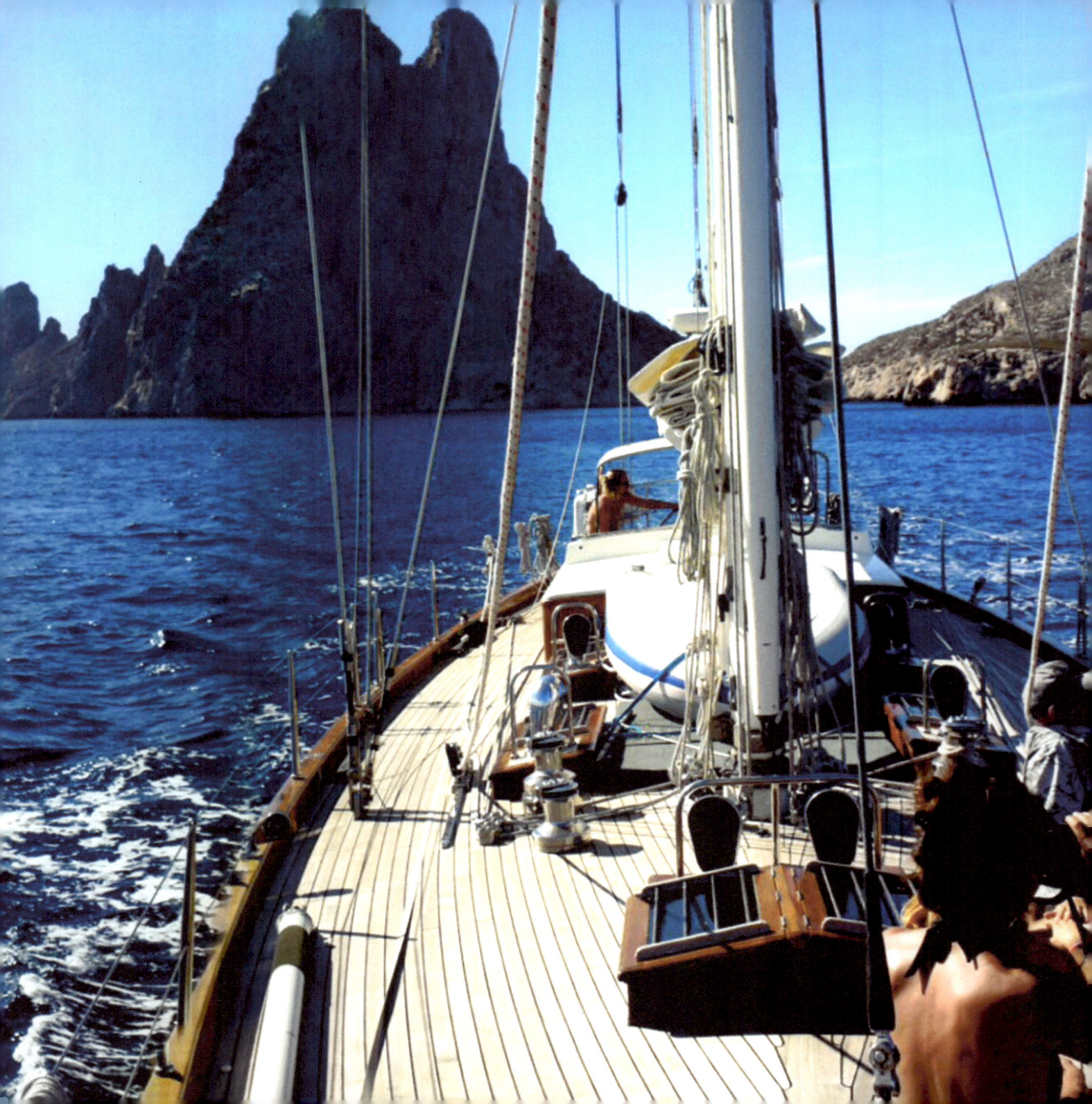

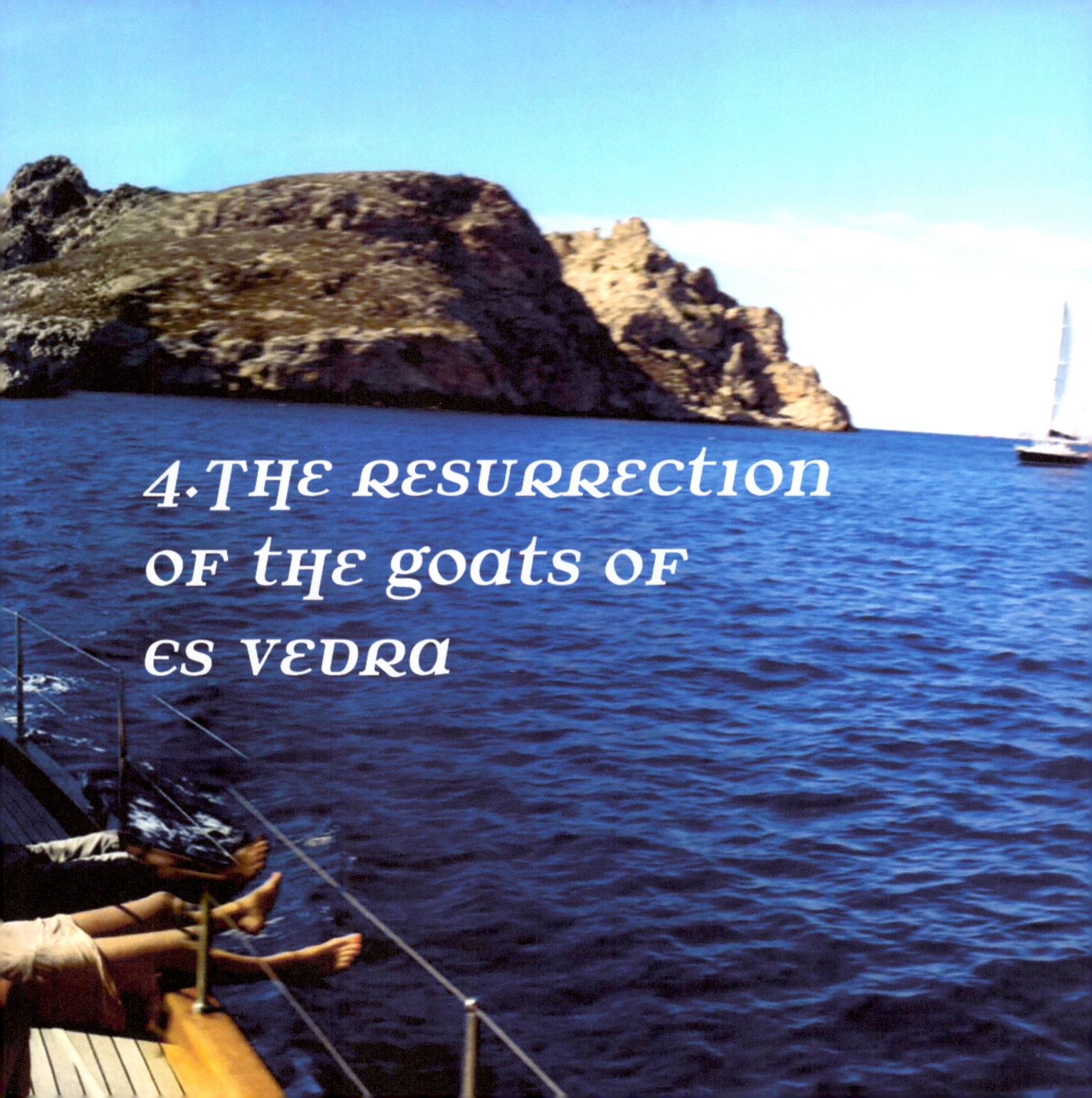

The sacred Rock Es Vedra is private property. Ibicencan families from the San Joseph area actually own parts of the Rock. Around 1992, they imported five female and one male goat. They replaced an older colony that had died. The new 'Cabra's de Vedra' multiplied to an estimated 40 to 50. As the story goes, once a year, the owners would shoot some goats and take them on their boats. Ibicencan people are well known to respect nature.

Coming near Es Vedra, chances were you heard bells of the goats coming down the slippery slopes to greet you. A sheer miracle to experience amidst the barren magical Vedra landscape. It made the Rock come alive and added some welcome innocence in contrast to its overruling power. Some people with fine noses claimed they could smell the native omnivores from far.

Es Vedra was not able to protect its grazing wild inhabitants.

In the morning of the 4th of February, 2016, environmental agents sailed over to Es Vedra and started shooting the terrified goats. By 2 pm it was all over. The bodies of the slaughtered animals were left where they fell. How did it come this far?

The Conseil of the Governments of the Balearic Islands, together with the local government, one day decided that the local heroes of Es Vedra had become a threat to its flora and fauna. Es Vedra has a vulnerable ecosystem, not much grows and thrives on its dry, often steep and eroded soil. Part of its unique habitat is the Eleanor's Falcon (Falco Eleanorae) and the famous blue subspecies of the green wall lizard (Podarcis Pityusensis Formenterae).
The blue lizard attracted National Geographic's attention. They send a team for a photoshoot on the very top of the Rock, using a 360 degrees panorama camera.

Apart from the blue lizard, the enigmatic slopes house some rare wildflowers. The Conseil decided the goat population ate too many wildflowers and threatened the Vedra ecosystem in general. Their time was up.

The people of Ibiza are animal lovers. They opposed the decision. Many expressed a desire and willingness to adopt some of the animals. The focus on the discussion soon pointed towards the argument not to shoot the poor animals, but to transport them from the Island. Even helicopters got mentioned in what could have become an epic goat rescue operation. The protester's numbers rose in the hundreds while discussions heated and grew intense. Sadly, the Conseil was convinced swift action was needed to save the unique Vedra flora and fauna. It set out a team of executors on that early February morning. They went the next day again to finish the job and to make sure no goat survived the slaughter.

Last year, I sailed close to Vedra, as I do every year with my neighbour. I remembered the joyful greetings of those innocent goats, the welcoming sounds from their bells. I was sad, feeling the Rock empty without its grazing friends. Only lizards, falcons, rats, mice and some insects remain.

When we sailed around the islet and got ready to set course home, I turned my head to have a last look at the green rocky slopes. My heart jumped a beat, noticing a young goat sticking it's weary head around the corner. It didn't make a sound, but it was undeniable there.

5. Artists and the Rock

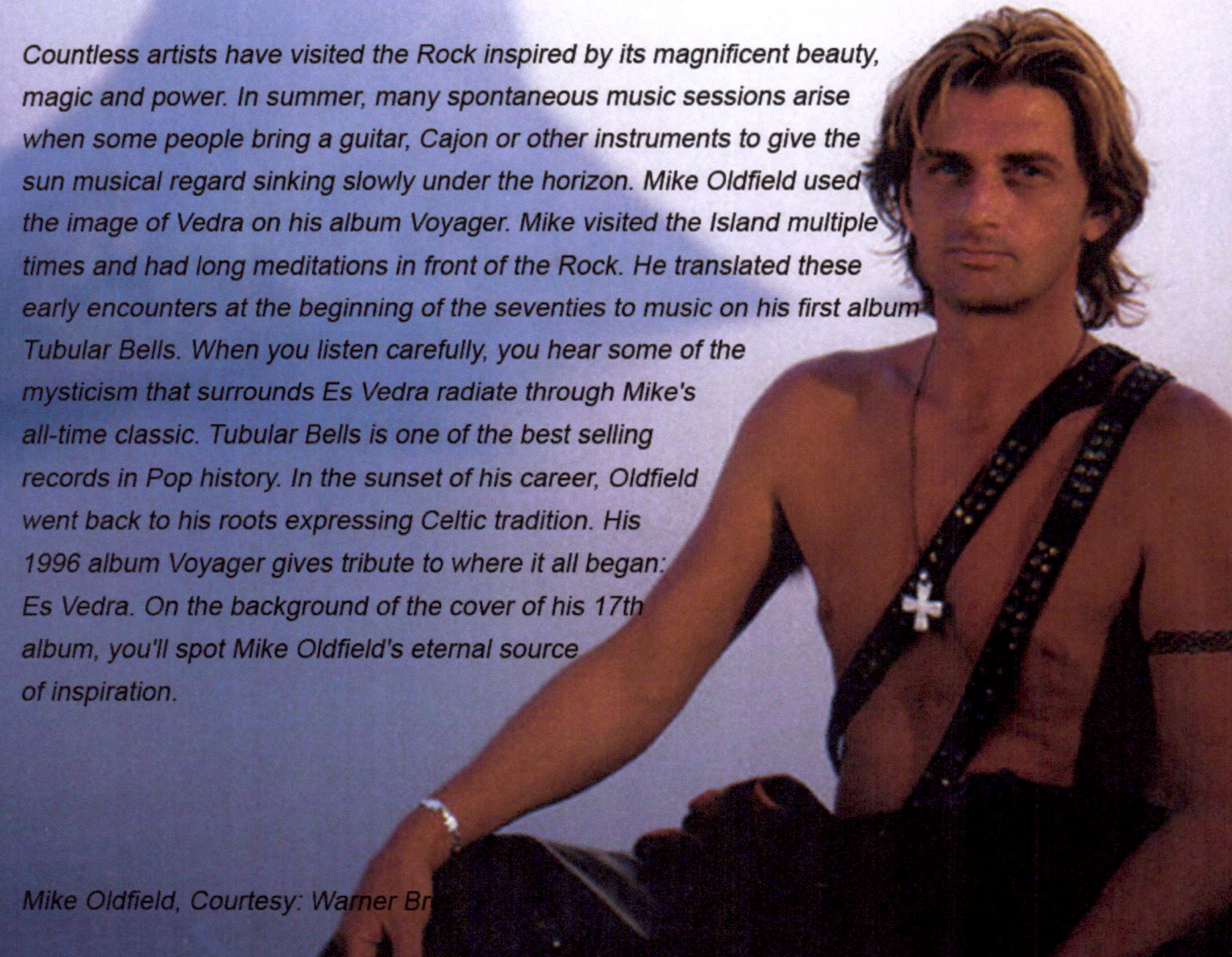

Countless artists have visited the Rock inspired by its magnificent beauty, magic and power. In summer, many spontaneous music sessions arise when some people bring a guitar, Cajon or other instruments to give the sun musical regard sinking slowly under the horizon. Mike Oldfield used the image of Vedra on his album Voyager. Mike visited the Island multiple times and had long meditations in front of the Rock. He translated these early encounters at the beginning of the seventies to music on his first album Tubular Bells. When you listen carefully, you hear some of the mysticism that surrounds Es Vedra radiate through Mike's all-time classic. Tubular Bells is one of the best selling records in Pop history. In the sunset of his career, Oldfield went back to his roots expressing Celtic tradition. His 1996 album Voyager gives tribute to where it all began: Es Vedra. On the background of the cover of his 17th album, you'll spot Mike Oldfield's eternal source of inspiration.

Mike Oldfield, Courtesy: Warner Br

Of beauty, sex and drugs

In the summer of '69, director Barbet Schroeder chose Ibiza for her cult movie 'More'. It was the peak of the hippie movement. Club night "Flower Power" just opened in Pacha two years earlier. London and Amsterdam were the epicentres of hippies bringing peace, love and marihuana to the world. Ibiza moved up fast on the hippy 'places to be' chart. A hot spot for folks expanding their consciousness, for enjoying music, dance and sensuality living from love and freedom.

It's not all flower power in Schroeder's movie. The story kicks off happily with a young couple arriving in Ibiza in summer, living in caves, smoking joints, reading existentialists, making love and swimming around nude. In winter, things get tough for the couple. Violence and drugs take over.

The script isn't mind-blowing. What makes this movie very appealing is the appearance of one of the biggest bands on earth: Pink Floyd. Their third studio album is the soundtrack for this movie. It's a mix of psychedelic influences, progressive Rock and soft melodies. The song 'Green is the colour', is Roger Waters favourite song on the LP. Did he get inspired by the millions of pine trees on Ibiza?

more
"toujours plus"

Barbet Schroeder · Klaus Grünberg · Mimsy Farmer

Raoul Hausmann

The small café Can Llorenç in San Joseph has a small plate on one of its white walls, barely noticed by the mostly local visitors. A tribute to photographer Raoul Hausmann, who often sat at one of the few tables. Hausmann, one of the co-founders of the Dada movement, was an anarchist and utopian. His experimental photographic collages, sound poetry and institutional critiques had a profound influence on the European Avant-Garde in the aftermath of World War I.

In 1933, he hastily fled Germany with his second wife and his lover and muse Vera Broïdo. The two women and the artist start a menage a trois. On the white Isle with its extraordinary light, not only he captures his muse on camera, but also the architecture represented in the famous country houses. Raoul photographs everyday life, nudes on the beach and meetings between men in the cafés of San Josep. With the rise of the Civil War in Spain in 1936, he is forced to leave his Mediterranean paradise.

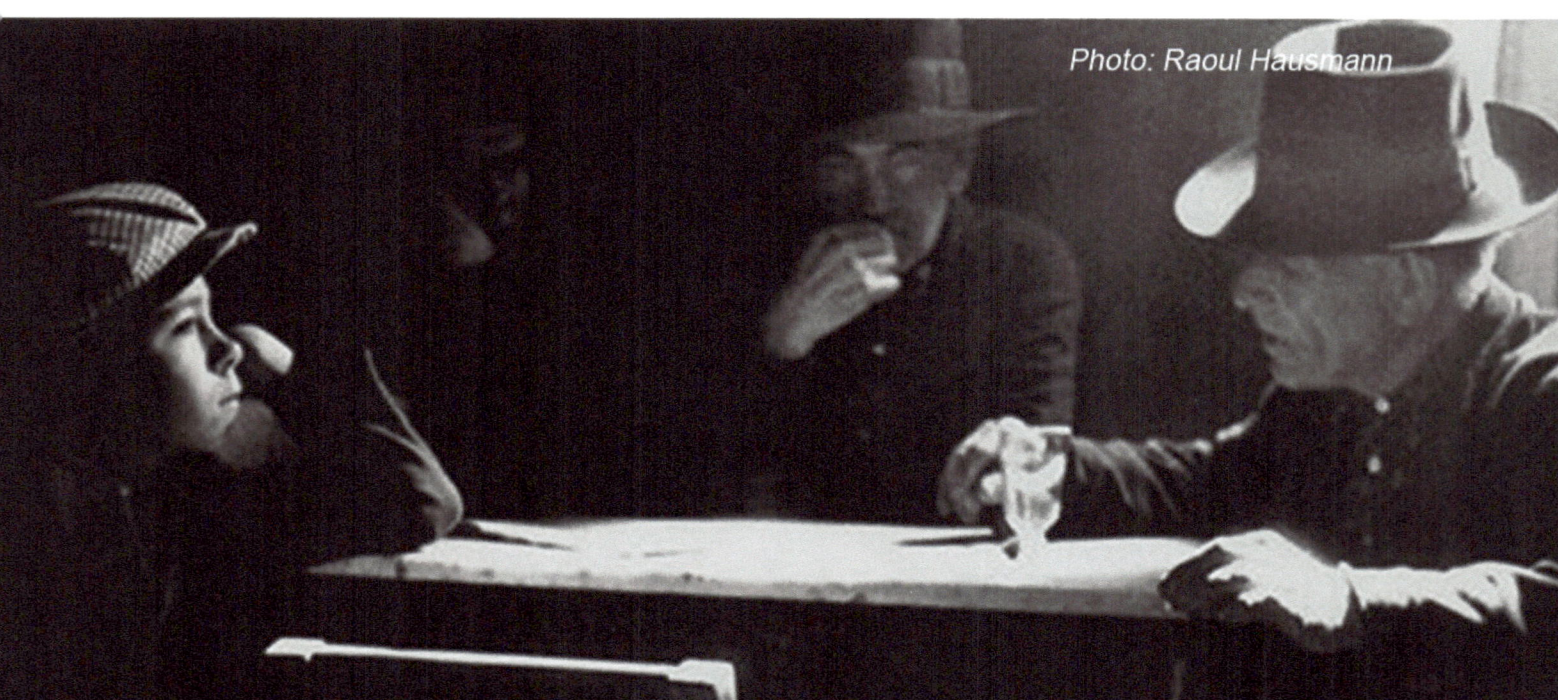

Photo: Raoul Hausmann

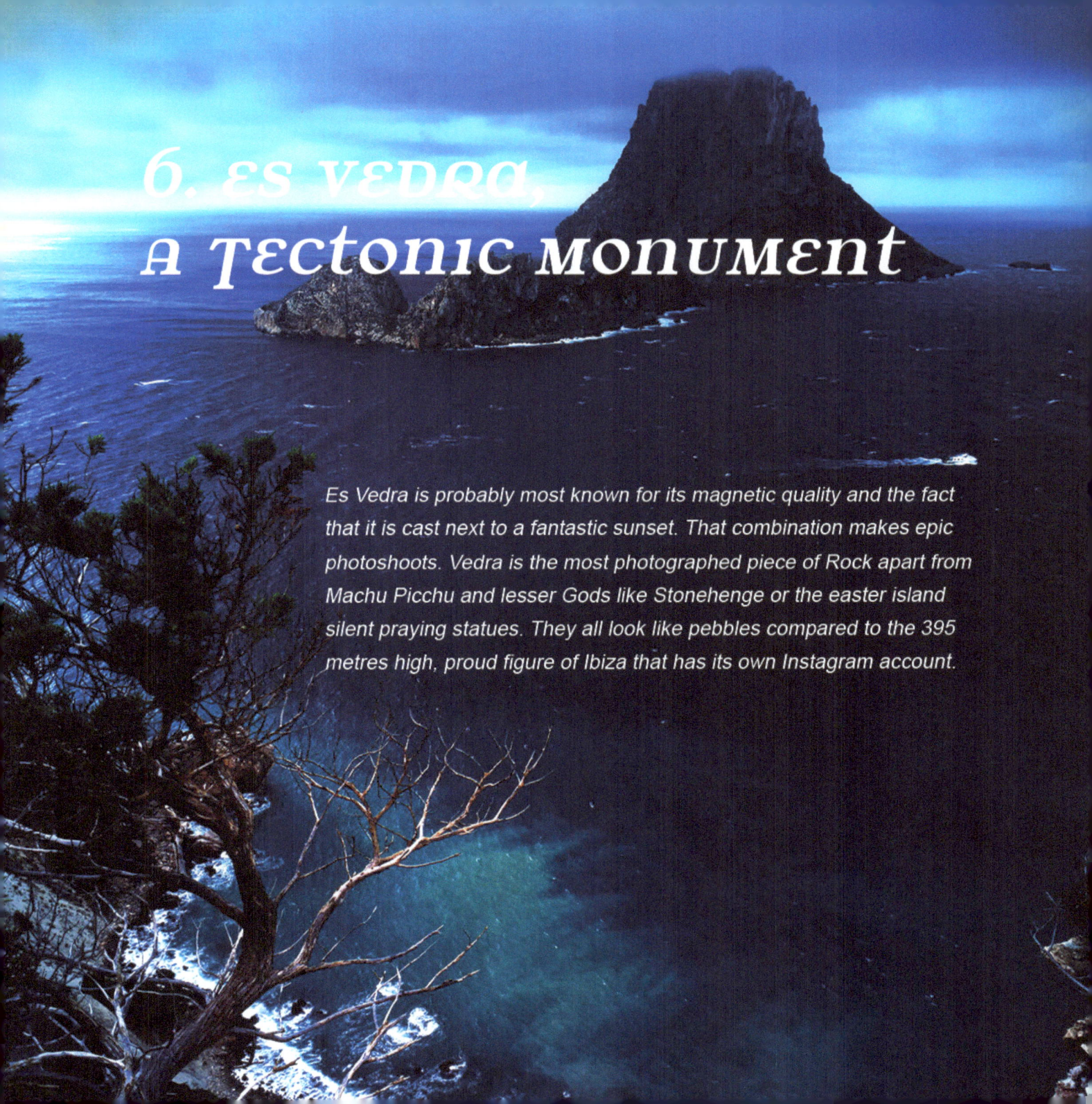

6. ES VEDRA, A TECTONIC MONUMENT

Es Vedra is probably most known for its magnetic quality and the fact that it is cast next to a fantastic sunset. That combination makes epic photoshoots. Vedra is the most photographed piece of Rock apart from Machu Picchu and lesser Gods like Stonehenge or the easter island silent praying statues. They all look like pebbles compared to the 395 metres high, proud figure of Ibiza that has its own Instagram account.

The shape of Es Vedra changes depending on what position or place you are. From the beach of Cala D'hort, you'll see the front of the sphinx and the side of Es Vedranell, the dragon in the water. The distance from the beach of Cala D'hort to the Rock is 1.5 miles or 2.4 km. My neighbour swam it in 1 hour and 8 minutes after daily training for 3 months. When you are sunbathing on the beach of Cala D'hort, and suddenly you get the idea to impress your mates or that sexy Spanish lady next to you: don't even try swimming to Vedra. Schools of jellyfish await you to give some shock and awe therapy, or 100-meter superyachts might cross your path. That's unfair competition. You hitting the bow of the ship won't even cause a ripple in the rosado served at the yacht's interior pool.

When you sail to Formentera from, let's say Porroigh or Salines, you'll see the Rock in its full length, and you'll understand the image of the lying sphinx. The best view, however, is when you come flying in from the north. First, you pass Mallorca, the plane descends, and when you're lucky and choose a left window seat, you get the best views ever over Es Vedra and a magical entree to the island. This is what you see

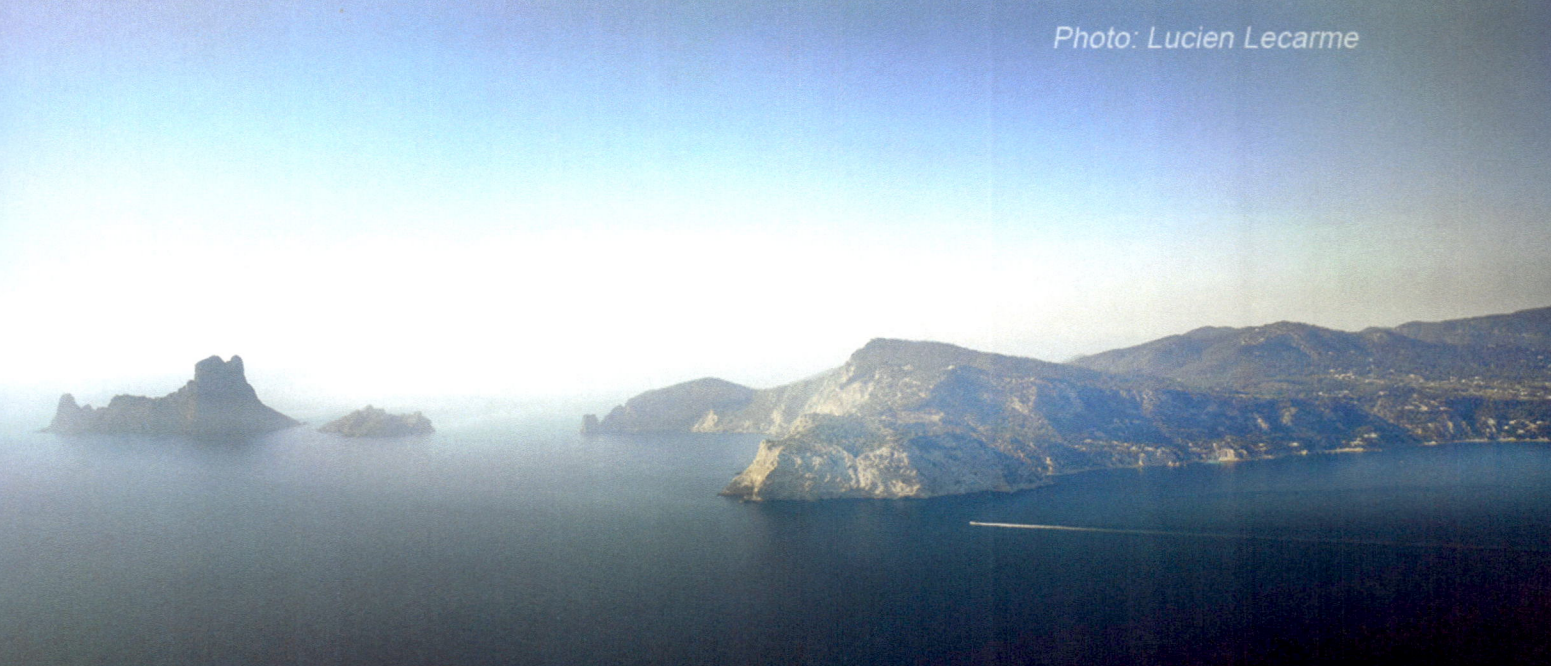

Photo: Lucien Lecarme

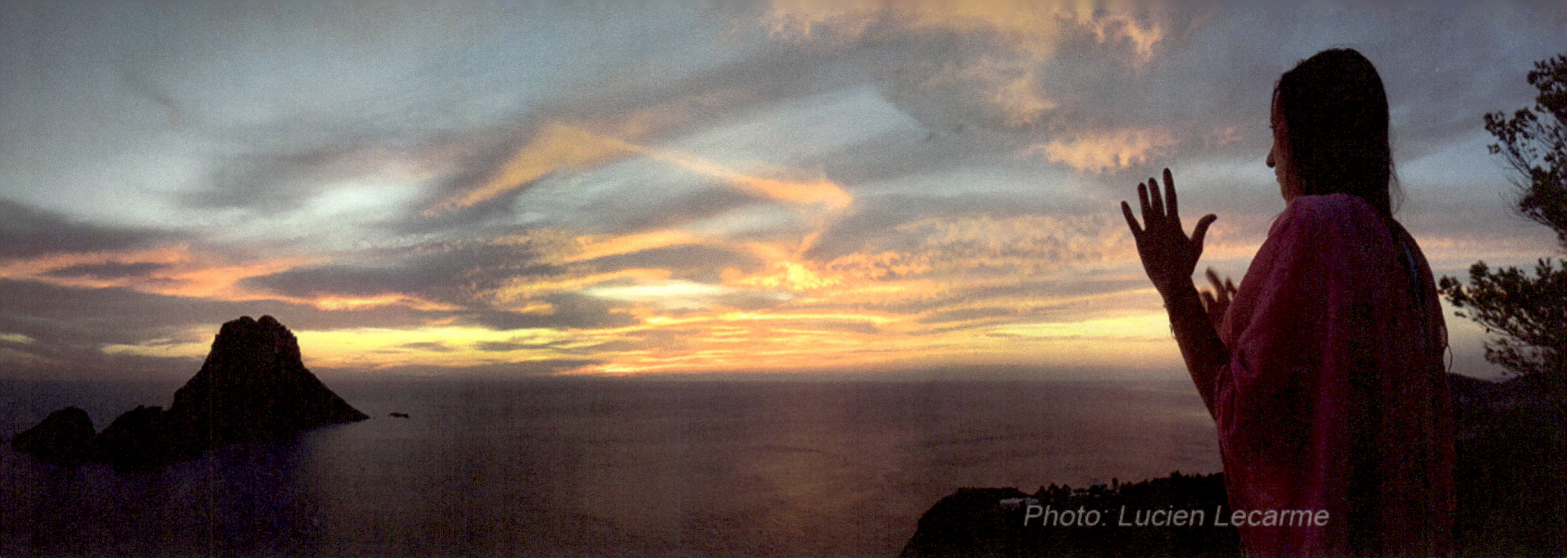
Photo: Lucien Lecarme

When we leave the fantastic view and all the stories that circle around Vedra like the seagulls carried by the wind behind, we end up with some fascinating geological information. How old you think the Rock is? Any guess is a good guess.

The Rock originates from an unimaginable distant past. The dawn of time when constant forces from the earth created and then split the massive Betica Mountain Range. This caused the formation of what we now call the Balearics. Further movements caused portions to shear and break away into smaller satellite islands like TagoMago, Es Vedranell and Es Vedra itself. The Rock has two peaks, the 381,53 meters high Picatxo de Tramuntana in the north, and the 375 m Picatxo de Migjorn in the south. Vedra formed a sheer 155 million years ago, no tourism back then.

Es Vedra consists of Mesozoic limestone. Here's the crazy part: No magnetic particles ever have been found in its accumulations. Now how to explain it's magnetism? Let's have a look at one of the oldest sciences in the world, from India: Vaastu. This forefather of Feng Shui teaches that specific shapes of landmass, arising in certain positions, and tilting towards specific directions, will become energetically loaded.

Add to this the power of myth. The Stonehenge stones are just rocks. Placed in a symmetrical circle form, they've become a legend. The tale gives the site power through the projection of people visiting the place, and the countless rituals performed by white-bearded druids and dancing Goddesses in the moonlight. Interesting theory, don't you think?

I just made it up. But it does make sense. As the storyteller of this story, I am allowed to let my phantasy run wild until some scientist comes and proves me wrong. I mean, Vaastu exists and is sturdy. I leave giving meaning to you, dear reader. When my theory is correct, your worshipping will add to its power, as this book will.

When we skip all the human stories surrounding Es Vedra, its raw, untamed, dark and light energetic quality is still there. I can feel it every day when I look at the Rock and take its energy into my system.

Can you feel it too?

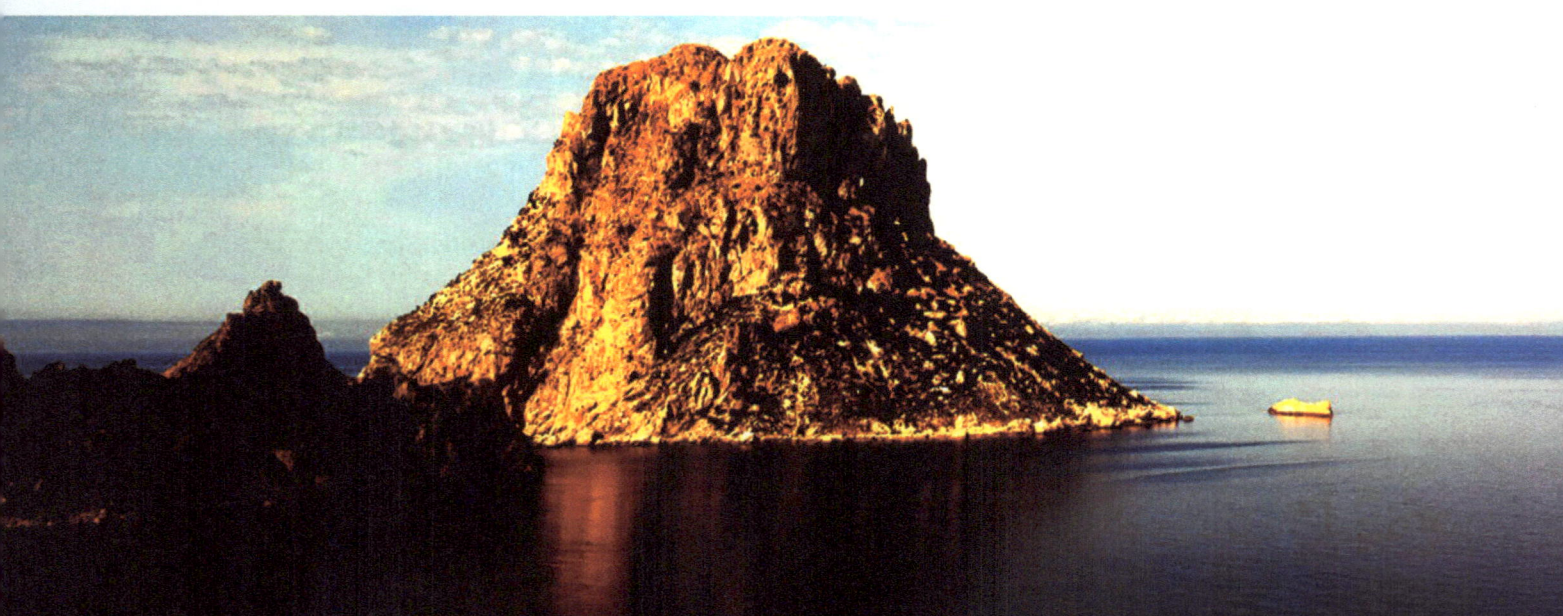

7. Spiral Dance

Rain drizzled from a greyish afternoon sky on October 21st, 2017. I'd guided a Dutch family to Atlantis, one of Ibiza's mystical destinations. When you haven't been there, Atlantis looks like men made rectangular structures, half above the sea and half beneath it. Hence the name Atlantis.

From above, the whole thing looks like Noah's Ark, ready to sail the seas and safe humanity. This ark will go nowhere since it is made out of sandstone.

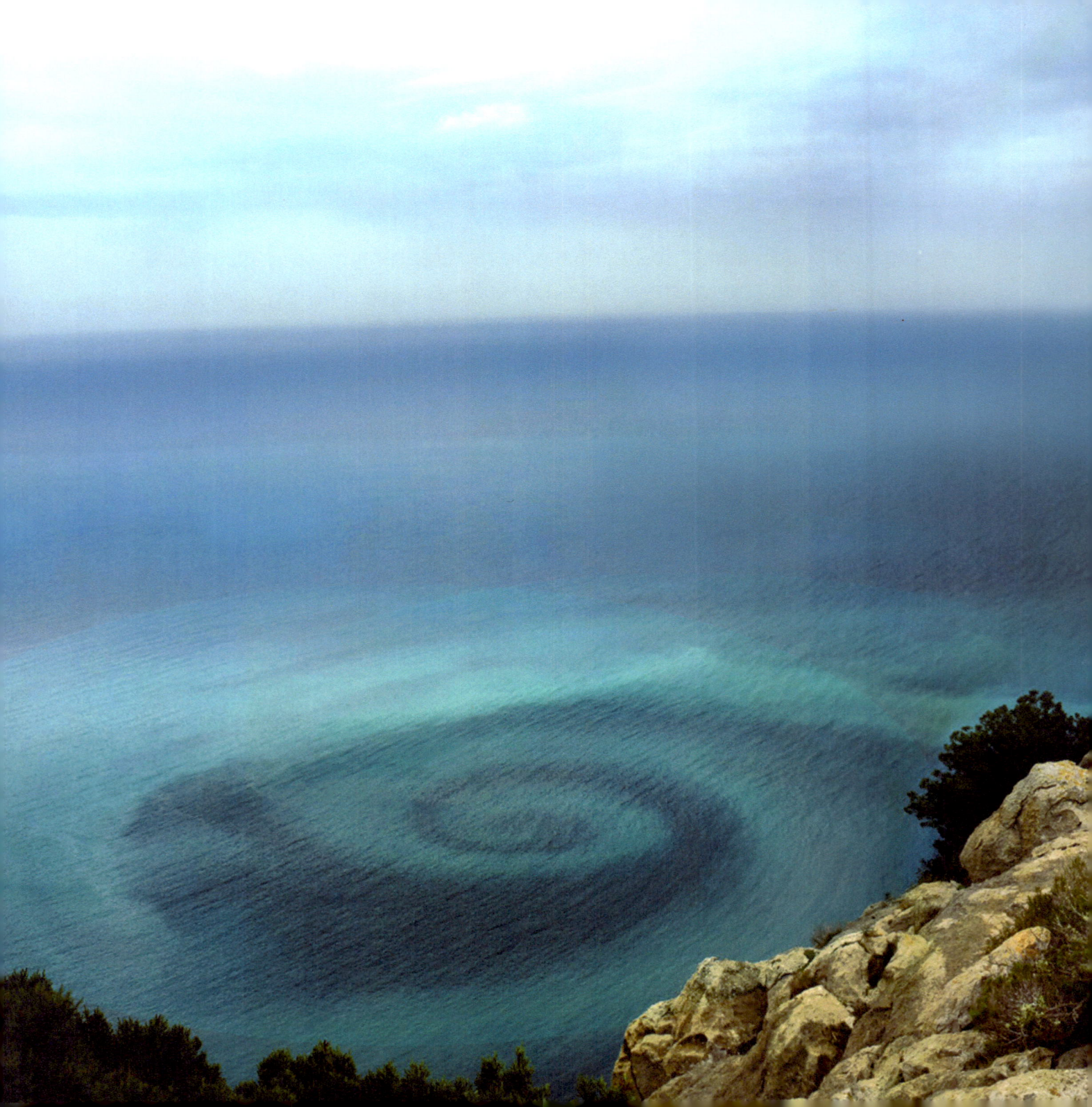

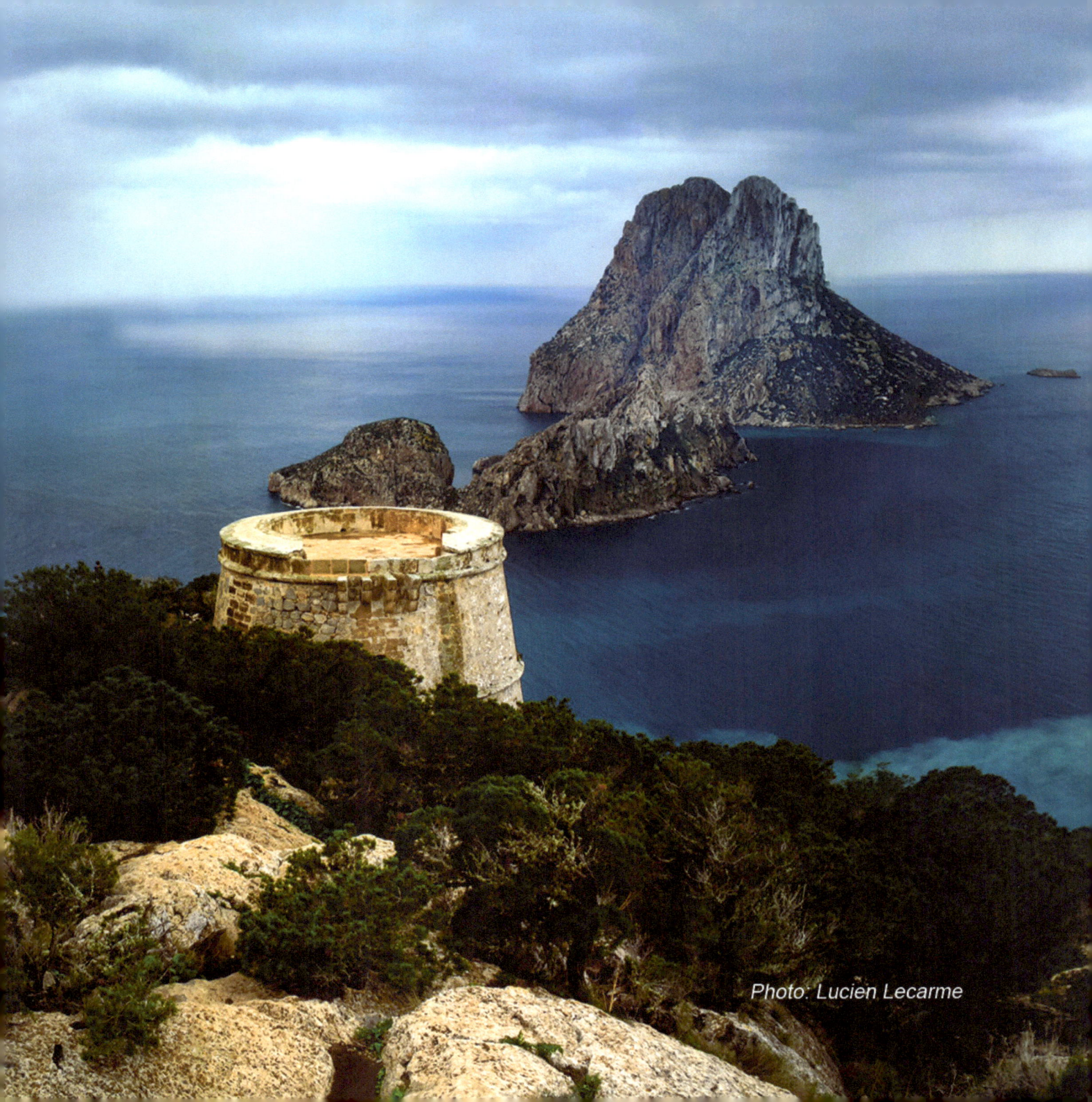
Photo: Lucien Lecarme

It is possible to enter the heart of Atlantis. When you find the secret passage, you'll experience very serene energy. There, I talked about the mystery of how the Phoenicians took out big blocks of sandstone to build the walls of Ibiza town with the same technology the Pyramids arose in Egypt. A technology unknown to mankind.

It was time to get ready for the big ascent. Going down to Atlantis is difficult for many, but going back up the small steep sand paths is an even more significant challenge.
Not for the kids, they loved it.
I invited the family to walk in the spiral and make an offering in the centre. I explained to them that this central shrine is a sacred place where they can let go of things that no longer serve their growth. It's like dying. I invited them to breath in deeply, and walk back spiralling embracing the birth and inviting something new in their lives.

When we left the spiral to make the unusual ascent from the backside to the Torre des Savinar, the pirate watch tower of Cala D'hort, we didn't know what big surprise was awaiting us.

Almost on the top of the hill, I turned to the left to take one last glance at Atlantis. What I saw next took all my breath away: A huge perfect spiral in the sea, at least 2 km wide. Exactly between Atlantis and Es Vedra. My brain could not place this image immediately, but my body and heart knew instantly, in a nanosecond. This was a miracle of nature.
A colossal present was given to us.

My photographer's instinct survived this energetic blast, and I quickly took out my Nokia 43 megapixel camera phone. I took that one shot. Then I turned around to the family and pointed at the miracle.

Yes, Yes, A spiral. Can we go home now?

Why didn't they see it? Or was it just tiredness? I decided to have a last look at this sheer miracle nature had just revealed to us, and guided the family home. Later I Googled 'Spiral in the ocean', and found nothing.

Ever since I published the photo, in exhibitions and as the cover photo of my debut novel "The Wisdom Keeper", people ask me for an explanation. Or does that spiral appear more often? What I did find with Google, was a postcard from around 1954, with the same spiral, on the exact same place. Nothing in between, no more images, Nada.

Of course, I can come up with some explanations. What about irritated algae that surface and form a spiral? What about different currents in the sea? It had been a rainy week and streams of greyish mud mixed with seawater. The location of the spiral was right at a place where two significant undercurrents meet.
All of this does not explain the utterly perfect form of the spiral. My best guess is sacred geometry. Why did Andres make that spiral there? What about the postcard from 1954?

A spiral is a vortex—a place of higher frequency and unique energy. Don't forget that we, humans, only perceive or can observe a tiny percentage of the electromagnetic spectrum of waves & frequencies. So much is hidden for our senses.

Let the legend remain.

Another story from the rock that meets the heart and not the mind.

8. A Spiritual Pull

From the dawn of time, Es Vedra has been surrounded by tales of miracles, legends and stories of the paranormal. From the first Ibicencan farmers and fishermen, to hippies and new agers seeking spiritual redemption, downloads or signs.

People use legends and stories to explain something that goes beyond science and what the mind can comprehend. Myths are a doorway to both our subconsciousness and the transcendental. They connect us back to our source. Myths, legends and fables often maintain a moral truth or lesson. You are at the right place to receive some truth at

Only a few places on earth coerce this human phenomenon of storytelling and myth-building. They are always places of extreme beauty, power and significance. Places where we pray and feel humbled by the presence of something much bigger, something our minds can't grasp, but our hearts feel. Es Vedra has it all.

One of the first fables coming from Ibicencan farmers living near Vedra is Es Gegant des Vedra, The Giant of Es Vedra. Ibicencan people call these legends Rondalles. The Giant of Es Vedra is the tale about two brothers who, to heal their father of an incurable illness, had to go to Es Vedra island to gather rock sapphire. By doing so, they had to confront a huge giant hiding in one of Vedra's many caves. The two brothers' wisdom, along with the help of sea urchins, managed to cripple the giant, and thus collect the samphire for the cure.

This fable speaks of courage and danger. I have heard some Ibicencan people speak with much respect about the rock, and they're not that eager to go there. For them, the place has a spell. It could be the spell of Es Gegant des Vedra, a story they heard when they were young. Everybody has his or her own way to fight with inner dragons.

Many feel a pull to Es Vedra that can't be scientifically explained. I am happy there is some magic left for the rock, some esoteric quality that speaks to the power of stories, not to the often dull wish of the mind to get explanations for everything.

This makes a visit to the rock a personal experience and sometimes even an adventure. You might like to visit for a kick-ass selfie, or maybe you'd prefer to sit silently in awe, sensing its energy, absorbing the silence and letting another amazing sunset land in your soul.

9. Other Stories from the Rock

Over the years, I've heard many stories about Es Vedra. From tourists and locals. These anecdotes are impossible to fact check. Hence they come from people's own experience. These modern-day fables about Es Vedra' proof' it's magic essence, its magnetic pull. Here are 2 of these stories, told to me years ago. They might have suffered from the storyteller's bias. Nonetheless, their essence remained captured.

The Three Lights of Es Vedra

Ibiza is home of the human design movement. One of its founders developed this modality on the island and taught it to one of the iconic characters that lived on the island: Lippy. In fact, Lippy was my neighbour for years, residing in some of the caves with a direct view on Es Vedra. In wintertime, Lippy would knock on my door at 7 AM, frozen to the bone.

Caves don't have central heating. We would share a modest but warm breakfast of porridge next to the fireplace. On one of these mornings, Lippy told me a revelation. Three distinctive bright lights had appeared to him that very same night, precisely in a triangle between Es Vedra and Es Vedranell. This, according to Lippy, was another time-space vortex with enormous healing abilities. After Lippy's visit that cold winter morning, I regularly stared at this exact same spot between the two rocks. The triangle of healing never revealed itself to me. I do, however, believe Lippy had a genuine experience, despite possible consumption of LSD, Mushrooms, San Pedro or a mix of these elevating medicines.

Stand Naked in the face of Utopia: Atlantis.

I love to tell you this story about Atlantis. In fact, this sacred cultural heritage deserves its own book! Atlantis, or Sa Pedrera, is around the corner of Es Vedra. One story especially sparked my imagination. Jonny Lee, co-founder of Last Night A DJ saved my life foundation, told me this story. In the sixties and seventies, Atlantis was reserved for hippies, and the odd celebrity admiring the sandstone hand made shapes. The curious visitors would make the steep descent bare feet, as a pilgrimage to sacred heritage. But not only bare feet.

The visitors stopped at a place called the Shiva Cave. A true sanctuary of soft eroded yellow sand covered by Tibetan flags. The 2 person cave is flanked by an impressive rock painting made by a Japanese Ibiza worshipper living in this cave for half a year. This image later appeared on the cover of the 11th Cafe Del Mar CD, while our Japanese friend didn't know about it. But that's another story.
The utter respect people had for this place was expressed through everybody taking off all their clothes before descending to Atlantis. People will appear naked in the face of God, and apparently in their descent to the lost city of Atlantis. This honouring shows an unprecedented level of worshipping these folks had for this place.

You only enter Atlantis as a child of God.

El Mirador

Beauty is in the eye of the beholder. It can't live without admiration. Es Vedra is one of the few rocks in the world that has groupies, an Instagram page and has been featured many times on the covers of magazines, books and as we have learned LP's. And it doesn't stop there.

Every single day in summer, hundreds of admirers gather on El Mirador, a flat piece of land in the middle of the lower cliffs (Cap Blanc) and the hill on which the pirate watchtower, el Torre des Savinar, is built. It's a real selfie hot spot, but don't get too close to the cliff. Every year some people fall off and die, taking their phones with them in the abyss.

What most of the tourists don't realize is that the Romans did the same from 123 B.C when they conquered the Balearics in their war against the Punic culture. I mean: celebrating. They honoured this victory on the exact same spot, and God only knows what happened. But you can be sure it stayed in Ibiza! A few solid big white rectangle rocks close to the cliff are the remains of a structure the Romans built on the Mirador, maybe the DJ booth?

The best moment to experience is just after the sunset. When the last piece of our orange life bringer hits the ocean and turns the day into night. When all people applaud in awe, expressing gratitude for yet another miraculous Ibiza day full of flow, extraordinary meetings and... stories.

Ibiza Stories.   ... This series will be continued...